I0154864

BEREFT
&
THE SAME-SEX HEART

Poems by Samuel E. Cole

Copyright © 2016 by Samuel E. Cole

Cover design: Nicole Bundy
Layout: Pski's Porch

All rights reserved. No part of this book may be re-
produced in any form by any electronic or mechanical
means including photocopying, recording, or informa-
tion storage and retrieval without permission in writing
from the author.

ISBN-13: 978-0-9978706-3-3
ISBN-10: 099787063X

for more books, visit Pski's Porch:
www.pskisporch.com

Printed in U.S.A

For Glenn

Contents

PARTNERSHIP

PARENTSHIP

BATTLESHIP

CITIZENSHIP

CENSORSHIP

OWNERSHIP

PARTNERSHIP

SOMEONE

                                        tell me
to ignore the evolving curiosity to attend
The Minneapolis Gay Men's Support Group
for dudes in the process of coming out:
                                        tell me
it's neither fabulous nor fun:
                                        tell me
to stop crossing off with a red pen
the week leading up to the first meeting
from my 365-days-of-bravery-calendar:
                                        tell me
no hot gay goes out on a Tuesday night:
                                        tell me
to wear dark apparel, vermillion times
droop, throw on labor-boots, don a
Potter-beard, spritz HULK cologne
from the Dollar Tree:
                                        tell me
being twenty-seven merits cooler titillation:
                                        tell me
to drive past the dilapidating red-brick
building with feminine-font letters
accosting a manufactured front door:
                                        tell me
paying for meter-street
parking is too straight-laced:
                                        tell me
to run away after glancing in the
room at twenty-one emphasized
haircuts sitting upright and round:

                                        tell me
this is not the kind of circle jerk to
which I've grown accustomed:
                                        tell me
to sit anywhere but across his polo-
tight torso and demiurge face:
                                        tell me
to not twinge when he conflates
DNA and castaway with less:
                                        tell me
to stop chanting his name on the drive
home, over and over and over (and over)
                                        tell me
of the enjambment in his smoothness:
                                        tell me
of the chamber madness in his glands:
                                        tell me
of the net drag in his self-regard:
                                        tell me
of the colorlessness in his rainbow:
                                        tell me
following him with uniform-routineness
will make me weak-jawed and cross-
eyed and land-lost a bazillion times over:
                                        tell me
he is not coursing a footpath to authenticity:
                                        tell me
he is not gooseflesh flaming across my skin:
                                        tell me
he is not bath salt and luminary and
urge and fjord and missiles and ass

and ten toes wiggling in the morning and
a gravel yawn peeing on the toilet seat and

a canyon sitting at the kitchen table
staring out the window like wet fog

trapped inside his father's raincloud.

THE CYCLE TO BECOMING A DISFIGURED MEMENTO

Raced by innovation to the carousel,
I mounted the kaleidescope-saddled horse

while you sat aristocrat-chest on a slick-
preen creamsicle carriage to the right,

grown men grandstanding cliques of
stork-size children and selfie-smirk

teenyboppers; dandies overriding dandiless
adolescence; labels refashioning cannot and

will not with can and will—the best route to take—
spectrum thirties breaking middle age protocol

with periphery stance expectancies
to hustle cameras and lean sideways

and curl back from hollow sidelines.
Twofold and thrice. Bounce and brisk. Like yay.

I tamed the stallion. You reigned in the coach.
Four more rounds? Hell yeah. Do you remember

my eye-brightness and honeymoon-chuckle jamboree
and zany fingerclaps at the elephant ear in your left

hand and mini-model carousel in the right:

now you can ride it whenever you want—
now you can turn the knob clockwise

to get things started—now it'll last for an
eternity—now it's yours for always and for keeps.

Squeezed like a weapon the morning
of our final descent, I ripped the heralding flag

from atop the canopy, threw shell-shock
curses against the wall, stomped shards

into scraps, impinging can and
will with cannot and will not

—the worst route to take—
limn thumbprints sifting through the

black and blue assortment, snapping like a
bloody knuckle my horse and your carriage.

LOGIC: THE (IN)VALID ARGUMENT

I am recuperating from misfortune.
If I am recuperating from misfortune, then I am mending.
Therefore, I am mending.

I am making the bed.
If I am making the bed, then I am awake.
Therefore, I am awake.

I am cooking food.
If I am cooking food, then I am eating.
Therefore, I am eating.

I am walking to and from the mailbox.
If I am walking to and from the mailbox, then I am outdoors.
Therefore, I am outdoors.

I am unpacking knick-knacks.
If I am unpacking knick-knacks, then I am decorating.
Therefore, I am decorating.

I am lighting candles.
If I am lighting candles, then I am in the bathtub.
Therefore, I am in the bathtub.

I am answering the phone.
If I am a answering the phone, then I am conversing.
Therefore, I am conversing.

I am television-marathon-binging on Naked and Araid.
If I am television-marathon-binging on Naked and Afraid,

then I am tuning in.
Therefore, I am tuning in.

I am mapping geography.
If I am mapping geography, then I am a surveyor.
Therefore, I am a surveyor.

I am sorry for cheating on our possibilities.
If I am sorry for cheating on our possibilities, then I am maturing.
Therefore, I am maturing.

I am lamentation scrapbooks.
If I am lamentation scrapbooks, then I am drained.
Therefore, I am drained.

I am crowd-surfing your web of familiarity.
If I am crowd-surfing your web of familiarity, then I am ensnared.
Therefore, I am ensnared.

I am a five-hundred square foot mudflat.
If I am a five-hundred square foot mudflat, then I am
cutting corners.
Therefore, I am cutting corners.

I am supposed to have one destiny but am forced to make another.
If I am supposed to have one destiny but am forced to make
another, then I am a blank slate. Therefore, I am a blank slate.

I am stepping in and out of woe .
If I am stepping in and out of woe, then I am modulation.
Therefore, I am modulation.

I am not in love with you.
If I am not in love with you, then I am not in love with you.

Therefore, I am not in love with you.

I am still in love with you .
If I am still in love with you, then I am still in love with you .
Therefore, I am still in love with you.

FIGHTING IN EVENING RAIN

Rave lightning erased our inky
shadows from the black tar.

Arcade thunder rumbled us into
tiny fractures trembling at the edge.

IQ TEST: SEPARATION MODULE

1. Which is the odd man out?

   ☹ ☹ ☹ ☹ ☹ ☺ ☹ ☹ ☹ ☹

2. What emotion is suggested at right?

3. Which word comes closest in meaning to feint?

   TRUTHFUL, SHAM, FAITHFUL, BLACKOUT, DECEIT

4. What word can be placed on the end of these words to
   form new words?

   taste
   color
   use   (_ _ _)
   heart
   faith

5. If man X dwells with man Y for 7,363,282.73 minutes, how
   many years is that?

   a. three   b. five   c. eleven   d. fourteen   e. nineteen

6. Which word means the fear of colors?

   a. HYPNOPHOBIA

b. CHROMOPHOBIA
c. POLYPHOBIA
d. HUEICKPHOBIA
e. HERPETOPHOBIA

7. SINGLE is to ONE as CIPHER is to:

a. TEN
b. HUNDRED
c. ZERO
d. TWO
e. FOUR

8. Add one letter, not necessarily the same letter, to each of these two words to make them synonyms.

RIVE   REAK

9. Which two of these words are opposite in meaning?

VAST, WEAK, LARGE, STURDY, GREAT, GRAVE

10. Find pairs of letters to form four, four-letter insects—one pair is not used.

AT	EA	LI
GN	CK	TI
CE	SO	FL

11. In how many ways can the word HOPE be read? Start at the central letter "H" and move in any direction.

```
              E
            E P E
          E  P O P  E
        E P O H O P  E
          E  P O P  E
            E P O
              E
```

12. What phrase is indicated below?

```
┌──────┐
│  v   │
│  r   │
│  o   │
│  e   │
│  ti  │
│  etg │
│ ntac │
└──────┘
```

13. Which word is most similar to DEJECTION?

TRIUMPHANT, DOWNCAST, RAGING, MISERABLE, PROSAIC

14. JASPER: GREEN
TURQUOISE: ?

      BLUE
      YELLOW
      ORANGE
      PURPLE
      RED

15. Insert two words that are anagrams of each other to complete the sentence. For example, she removed the **stain** from her new **satin** dress.

A _____ paper-crafter, the man sent his separated self a handmade "with-sympathy" greeting card, because after seven months of not receiving one from friends or family, he knew it wasn't going to happen. Whenever the man thinks about this, tears _____ from his eyes and dribble down his cheeks.

16. Which two words have opposite meanings?

GREGARIOUS, SARCASM, TRIBULATION, HAPPINESS, MOCKERY

17. Simplify to find x:

$$\frac{-7 \times 3 \times 2}{3 \times 2 \times 7} = x$$

18. There are only five regular solids with symmetrical faces. Which one of these has twenty faces?

a. ICOSAHEDRON
b. DODECAHEDRON
c. CUBE
d. TETRAHEDRON
e. OCTAHEDRON

19. Insert a word that finishes the first word and starts the second.

LAND		ACRE

20. Make one word using all nine letters.

SCOOP HERO
clue: sign

21. Find a twelve-letter animal made of two six-letter words – one word inside, one word outside.

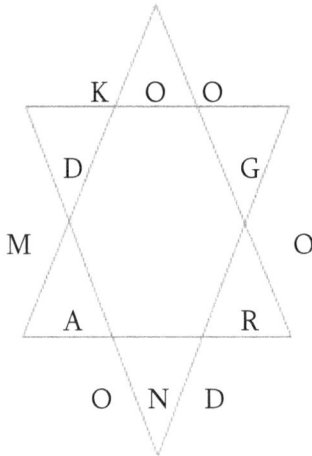

22. Which two words are similar in meaning?

INFORM, RENASCENCE, WELCOME, REBIRTH, DISPARAGE

23. Which word means the same as SOPHISTRY?

TRICK, SELFISHNESS, RIGHTEOUSNESS, CARELESSNESS, HABERDASHERY

24. Which number should replace the question mark?

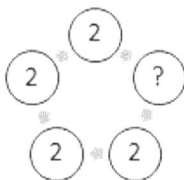

25. True/False

I miss sorting through our mail,
my name tumbling over yours.

***

Use the following scoring table for the test:

Score	Rating
25-23	Exceptional: you clearly understand separation
22-20	Excellent: you are keenly aware of separation
19-17	Very Good: you grasp the concept of separation
16-14	Good: you are becoming more cognizant of separation
13-11	Average: you are getting much closer to separation

Answer key: 1. Happy Face 2. Emptiness 3. Sham 4. "Less" 5. Fourteen 6. Cromophobia 7. Zero 8. Rive(n) (B)reak 9. Weak/Sturdy 10. Flea, Tick, Gnat, Lice - [SO] is not used 11. Twenty-eight 12. Can't Get Over It 13. Downcast 14. Blue 15. Master/Stream 16. Tribulation & Happiness 17. One 18. Icosahedron 19. Mass 20. Horoscope 21. Komodo Dragon 22. Renascence: Rebirth 23. Trick 24. Two 25. True (and False).

REVOLUTION IN PROGRESS

I know it's a problem. I admit it.
Pleading to meet once a week,

      maybe twice

—three times a charm, no?—
for a burger, a latte, a game of

Jenga, a little Battleship,
an ear, an eye, a mid-way point

between the bomb-dust remoteness
of my see-spot-sit in open recollections

and your see-spot-run in covert successions
arriving   later and   later

leavingfaster&faster
so busy, can't stay long, gotta go.

I suspect the *going* is to him,
though I do not ask, as I cannot

answer to his name, nor can I
stand up to the flight path with

which your smile catches air
when I ask if your bliss. Is.

      I remember when my name made you skip.
      I understand freshness keeps you going.

I see the rebirth of an essence ascending in color.

Goddamn it.

You've shed every sleeve of my impact.
You've adopted a new timer, lexicon, velocity, and aroma.

You've maneuvered into a proportion of
stratosphere I will never reach,

terminally stranded to our germ collection
growing still in my peripatetic arboretum.

What do you want and make it quick.

      Every declaration I'd performed sprints off field.
      Every compliment I'd groomed lurks backstage.
      Every inscription I'd authorized rewrites its own side.

Since when did you become speechless?

      My friends keep defining insanity, again.
      My family keeps defining disparity, again.
      My heart keeps defining finality, again.

*I don't eat burgers. I hate coffee. Jenga's weird. And
Battleship's for kids. Those are your things. Not mine.*

You leave before I can plead with you to stay.
You squeal away and scatter chameleon pollution.

You don't reply to Snapchat.
You let every phone call fizzle at the bottom of voicemail.

Figures.

> I rub a hand over the imperfections in the wall.
> I watch a series of cars pull in and back out.
>
> I pack up the burger, the latte, Jenga, and Battleship.
> I know your ears are mute to my levels.

It's just when you're with me,
I know you're not with him,
at least not in person.

ONLY THE LONELY

Even on shower days, I backflop in my

seething chair & shoot death-eye lasers
at the poorly tacked speaker booming the sheetrock,

plastic dandruff vaulting from its cheap

synthetic husk,

& press play, one-hundred decibels,

sinking like a stingray in saltwater

love songs drowning the shallowness of

our swimming charade,

every bombast ballad & casting crowns
still broken together & one celeb-tongue

tenor crooning *if you need me*

call out my name. So I call. Scream.
Bounce against brine & gather nose bubbles

transforming at the surface

your watermark impression.

FINAL CHORE

The house is manic in mid-summer tidy-up.
We're stereo-humming with Tegan and Sara.
Swiffers, 409, and lightbulbs are streaming live.

The living room is in the kitchen.
The kitchen is in the dishwasher.
The dishwasher is gurgling on uber-rinse.

Three hours in. One hour to go. We're good. So good.
I tickle the duvet and spank the pillows.
The music halts. Dishwasher, too.

My stomach knots. My posture shrivels.
I am not one to terminate. You are a fast hiatus.
I am not one to relax. You are a quick unwind.

I am hardwood maple. You are softcover pulp.
I am broom and dust pan. You are cobwebs and dust mites.
I am glued by dexterity. You are unhinged by stringency.

I did not see this chasm in the beginning.
I find you in the den, in my mother's chair
—a gift my father gave upon her passing—

arms dangling from the cherry spindle, Norwegian
chin and Italian eyes flung low. Haunting.
You are a thinker so I know you are thinking.

I do not pry. It is unwise to stretch your
boundaries with stingers and claws.

You are saddened so I know you are sad.

Tears burnish rosewater cheeks,
salmon-thin lips, and a nose that
can point me in any direction.

I want to soothe you, to crystallize my appointment,
to reaffirm the choices I've made by showing
you the dimensions of my mother's chair.

> See the fissures: the discoloration: it's still beautiful:
> Turn it upside down: tweak the springs: test it: it's still
> valuable:
> Run a hand over the fading legs: pluck the scrim in the seat:
> it's still purposeful.
> Press it against your chest: embrace the vibrations:
> it's still perfect.

You shoo me away so I know you want me to go.
You close the garage door so I know you want me to stay.
You return with an armful of blue

totes and a roll of packing tape
which you set on my mother's chair,
weeping for me and holding out for you.

THE STRIKE(R) & THE S(P)ELL

The (s)tart.

The cream of your s(k)in.
The loot of your s(l)ender.
The flash of your star(e).
The lag of your s(w)allow.

The (s)table.

The stream of your s(m)ears.
The boot of your s(t)ate.
The dash of your sp(i)rit.
The wag of your sham(e).

The s(t)op.

The gleam of your (s)hit.
The soot of your s(l)unk.
The brash of your (s)pine.
The brag of your s(p)ort.

The (s)old.

The scream of your (s)trap.
The moot of your s(h)ot.
The stash of your ton(g).
The crag of your d(r)ug.

The sp(l)it.

MISSING YOUR BIRTHDAY

No cake with tapers
to enflame your whoosh.

No gingham from Old Navy
to unfetter your hips.

No shindig with shrimp
to redden your hands.

No humor from Hallmark
to rekindle your tweet.

No ballroom with friends
to swell your tango.

No collage of family
to banner your beams.

No tickertape with confetti
to sparkle your caravan.

No playlist from funk
to disco your shimmy.

No cuddle with pecks
to haven your bulk.

No scrub from bleach
to brighten your loft.

No bedtime with manor
to reverie your ages.

PARENTSHIP

ANOTHER DOWNTOWN GREAT-AWAKENING TENT REVIVAL EXTRAVAGANZA

Her pinned-up wears rollicked in whirlwind hysteria:
crimson lipstick spewing Pentecostal

tongues, rosy Lee Press On nails raising glory's
marquee, black stilettos twirling the hem

of a cerulean-billow poodle skirt the length of
an altar call—my teetotaler mother

set adrift in an intoxicating trance by
a roving zealot's anointing hands

thumping her forehead with so
much Trinity, her teeth chattered

like a chorus line sloshed on
spasmodic rigidity. I sat quiet in the

front row. Hypnotized. My father, off
milking the suds of his kickbacks, was AWOL.

Mosquitos & ants & fireflies were invading the lanterns.
The sheer-blouse pianist wore corkscrew ringlets.

The engorged multitude was praying volumes
of provincial frenzy. Everything was stirring.

But me. The only one not under the spell.
The only one spooked like boo when she fell

prone to thrash & screech
& shudder & swoon & yelp.

What if she broke a hip?
What if she never came back?

During daytime calm, she unwound in bed,
a hodgepodge quilt pulled up to her jowl,

a dark-brown Bible banning her eyes from
trailing my sweat pant legs in flux between

the bedroom doorway and the foyer window
—damn cobalt sky—damn gassy-divination-clowns

messing with another three (in)sane moons.
Why couldn't she skip in sunlight? Why

couldn't she be under the influence of me?
Who was she trying to excise? I had to know,

jogging beside her to the weed-clay stage, yielding
disbelief in Deuteronomy 19:19—*You Must*

Purge The Evil Among You—she untangled my
clasp and vanished into stratum fervor

I was not believer enough to acquire or
scramble or cloak my losses around her skirt

or immerse my gravity into her thoughts or soar
the altitude her faith endeavored to peak,

take me with you, please,

retracted by an usher who held my waist at
at the brink of sundown while God's emissary

converted every impure notion, misdeed, and neurosis—

Is this who she was? Who we were?

milquetoast flaws in a cryptogram my pre-
adolescence couldn't unjumble the network

of Moses-fables from the mystery of Primate-fact
affixed to my mother's fascination

with Jesus-men, glutton personalities who
told her to drink, drink, drink from a pearly-gates

cask & surrender to The Savior who created &
escaped & reprised the best killing ever.

PATRIARCHLESS

We climbed trees behind the patio.
Roared at the summit.

I love his first impersonation
& dislike his second act.

I admire his orchard turnout
& renounce his marginalization.

I should not want to see
his nose hairs again.

I should not want to touch
his chainsaw scar every day.

He is my hammered father.
I am his nailed son.

He is my tear-duct encryption.
I am his toe jam jiggers.

We jockeyed dragons in the pasture.
Swam laps in the lagoon.

I'm thirty-five feet stumbling against his
imprisoned stargaze eclipsing my penchant holes.

He's seventy-six millennia backtracking from my
turncoat hogwash mocking his enraptured gospel.

I rebuke his guardianship absenteeism.
He reprimands my childhood reverberation.

"Hell can taste your cadaver, dear daddy-o."
"Heaven can smell your cinders, dear sonny-boy."

I try to persuade him with jurisprudence,
poetry, Instagram, and resemblance.

He tries to persuade me with Calvinism,
prose, Polaroids, and metamorphosis.

I t-shirt Ethridge, Tom of Finland,
Mapplethorpe, and Maddow.

He workbooks Osteen, Saul of Tarsus,
Kinkade, and O'Reilly.

We're possessed by barbarity. Enmity.
Dehydrated. Blood-bruised. Nits.

We swung at SunnyBrook Park.
Jumped rope nicking the sand.

I can shake lifestyle
objections from my eyelids.

I can ingest epoch neglect
without slander.

I can stop blocking phone numbers,
addresses, luggage, and pores.

Can he?

Why must we

continue through swift cuts and
sharp screens to score signature

discontent into layered armor
weary of felled battle grounds.

We held hands at church.
Sang loudly for canticle foundations.

GROWING MILD TO WILD TO AISLED IN A PASTORAL COUNTRYSIDE

Some parents lie. To children. Doppelgängers. Like me.

Turn 5.
Convince 5 God's life-creed for 5 is to become
an evangelical pastor.
Tell everyone.
Add embellishment rhetoric as proof of divine authentication.
: anointed by the Holy Spirit
: sanctioned by streets of gold
: endorsed by
~~amazing grace~~
~~the old rugged cross~~
~~a mansion on a hill~~
CROWN HIM WITH MANY CROWNS!

Turn 6.
Coax 6 to rigorously practice Lord-Almighty-verses
on dairy cows grazing in prairie grasses
flanking a manure pile behind a red barn.
Condemn every free-range (and free-will) proclivity.
Ring the cowbell and bring in the herd (and the sheaves).
Repeat sermon until bovine are redeemed. Or butchered.
Forgive hedonistic red heifer that kicks
dad's ribs and sneezes in mom's face.
Never forget.
Tell everyone.

Turn 7.
Unwrap Holy Bible.
Make a wish: puppy, any color, slightly used is fine.

Admonish 7 with pointed finger, dogs DO NOT go to heaven.
Nor do cows, because animals are soulless, silly goose.
But if dogs and cows don't have souls, why preach
conversion?
QUESTION NOTHING!
Play wise man #2 in church Christmas pageant.
It's not Old Frankenstein Makes Sense to Her.
It's Gold, Frankincense, and Myrrh. Retard.
Tell no one.

Turn 8.
Unwrap Holy Bible thesaurus.
Make another wish: one Sunday free of church, or a
Wednesday night will do.
Make 8 bring Bible and Bible thesaurus to school and
proselytize (similar meaning to convert and evangelize)
unsaved classmates, teachers, lunchroom ladies,
and that sicko janitor Judas, who better stop smooching men
in the street.
Suspect (similar to accuse) everyone of raging sinnerdom.
Leave Bible and Bible thesaurus underneath the bed four days
a week.
Tell no one.

Turn 9.
Unwrap summer Bible Camp brochure located in
the boondocks
without a lake, firepit, bicycle trail, or snack times.
Abandon wishing: forgo wishing altogether: fuck wishing.
Browbeat 9 to join the church Bible quiz team that
practices for two-hours after every three-hour sacrament.
Incorrectly answer as many questions as possible
at every Bible quiz competition in Brainerd, MN.
Blame incorrect answers on being over-churched.

Rescind being over-churched when parents mention more
church as cure.
Steal the neighbor boys' Vikings-purple moped
and speed through town after town (after town)
until sun and fuel and resolve run out.
Rediscover the art of kneeling.
Confess malevolence (similar meaning to foul and vile).
Rededicate life-creed to God and God alone.
Tell everyone.
Cuss life-creed to shit and to hell below.
Tell no one.

Turn 10.
Coerce 10 to begin separating humanity into categories.
Instill demeaning labels and pulpit-addled stereotypes
: avoid hyper-Mary Catholics.
: pity liberal-loose Presbyterians.
: censure cult-craze Mormons.
: remind skullcap-Jews.
: abhor Muslims, Buddha, Mohammad, and Asians.
Punish 10 by willow switch any divergence from
saintly dress code, decent speech pattern, religious
zeal, and seamless excellence,
BOYS DON'T CONDUCT THEMSELVES WITH FLAIR!
NEVER WEAR FLAIR! FLAIR IS SNARE!
Accept only those who believe and do
the exact same things as you.
Loathe worldly collusion, dissimilarities, and juxtaposition.
Love thy Caucasian, Middle-class, Midwestern, Christian, Re-
publican, Hermeneutic-Thumpity-thump-thump Compatriot.
Blend in with school popularity without conforming to pop-
culture Satanism.

LISTEN WEIRDO, WE DON'T WANT YOU

Sit on the bedroom floor and sigh in the dark.

Remove crucifix above desk.

Hang it back up.

Thank God for not being born in Yemen or Ghana or Fargo.

Imagine a happy life in Australia with a pet kangaroo named Freedom.

Dream of an even happier life in Norway as part of The Royal Family.

Cry a little.

Tell no one.

Turn 11.

Threaten 11 with Nintendo prohibition and withheld movie-munchie-money

> unless 11 volunteers at church as usher, preschool mentor,
> cantor, envelope licker, pew duster, stair sweeper, lobby
> vacuum attendant, and Bible quiz President, VP
> (and secretary).

Realize that salvation without good works is punishable by manipulation.

Submit to obedience.

Suppress bitterness.

Robotically recite religiously right responses regularly. Repeat.

Hurl crucifix in the manure pile behind the red barn.

Swap the word God with the word fart in both testaments.

Laugh out loud. Switch fart with booger. And howl.

Scream fuck with sonic silence.

Steal fifty dollars from the offering plate. Then seventy-five.

Turn felt-Jesus upside down on the Sunday school felt board.

Sing off-key during The Lord's Prayer. And Benediction.
Lick only half of the building-fund campaign envelopes and
barely tap down the seals.
Dust church lobby as if there's nothing to dust.
Sweep only every other stair.
Vacuum around the tables and chairs.
Continue being President (similar meaning to
commander and chief, minus Air Force One).
Continue being Vice-president (similar meaning to
second rate and first loser).
Continue being Secretary (similar meaning to
scribe and waxwork).
Deem Jesus, during youth group, a most fantastic antagonist.
Tell no one.
Moniker Jesus, during an episode of Love Boat, Captain Hat
Trick.
Tell no one.

Turn 12.
Masturbate hourly.
Think about sex minutely (and acutely).
Envision masturbating with cute boys at school.
Repent.
Envision masturbating with cute girls at school.
Repent.
Question everything.
Cry a little more.
Tell no one.

Turn 13.
Strong-arm 13 to spend summer VACA teaching
mentally-handicapped children at Bible camp how
to pray with articulate vowel sounds and hit a huge,

inflatable beach ball over a clothes line in the dirt.

Continue wearing neck cross and speaking Jesus jargon.

Exhume Jonathan and David from the book of Samuel.

Read and recite: the soul of Jonathan was knit to

the soul of David,

and Jonathan loved him as himself.

Really?

Two boys. Best friends. Knit to the soul. Loving Jesus. No way.

Ask Pastor Holm for enlightenment (similar meaning to

insight and data).

Bad idea.

"You do know the difference between male homosociality and
male homosexuality?"

Diary homosexuality (similar meaning to same-sex attraction,
homoeroticism, gay, queer).

"It's the most abominational sin of all the abominational sins,"
Pastor Holm says.

"I don't believe abominational is a word."

"I don't believe normal boys ask questions about
abominational sins."

"I completely agree. Thanks for being

such a wise man of God."

Bite fingernails. To bloodlines.

Sit on the bedroom floor and copy the dark.

Shout, solo, It's not fair, so what am I supposed to do?

Ponder parallel opposites: If God is yes and gay is no than I am
no and God is cruel.

Study homophobia (similar meaning to contempt, antipathy,
hostility, bigotry, disavow, hatred).

Cry a little more.

Fist punch the pillow.

Curse Genesis to Revelation.

Tell no one.

Turn 14.

Torment 14 into finding a sweet, petite girlfriend.

Find it. Hate it. Lose it. Find it again. Hate it again. Lose it again.

Fight alone a fierce inner-battle raging like a lost war between emerging self-realization and parent's expanding godliness expectations.

Find it again. Hate it again. Lose it again. "If I'm not right then I must be wrong."

Reject girls and boys and testosterone and estrogen and sex and masturbation and fitting in.

Try to disremember Pastor Holm's abominational bias.

Try to imagine the world as a heartbeat pulsing with reception.

Take comfort in Jonathan. And David. And being knit to the soul.

Become silently open-minded.

Become openly petrified.

Don't cry. Or scream. Or wish.

Just pray it away. Day after day. And collapse.

Tell no one.

Sleep 15 Fissured.

Binge 16 Numb.

Lie 17 Obscurity.

Worry 18 Worthlessness.

19 (similar meaning to investigation and coagulation).

Keep 20's going to church after quick-tricks at rest areas, bookstores, and the WWW.

Self-hate. Self-injure. Self-schmelf.

Buy a Spartan Swiss Army knife.

Wear long angora and leer at everyone's surveillence.

Obsess over Jonathan and David. Can it be so easy? So open? So real?

Cringe when pastor (after pastor) yells, "Homosexuals are Satan's most perverted minions."

Cry a little more.

Shiver.

Tell no one.

Allow 30 to believe love teems with David (similar meaning to GFJ), the hot giant-killer.

Buy David a stuffed kangaroo named Freedom.

Give to and take from David. Mostly take. Some give. Shit.

Piss off everyone (similar meaning to parents, siblings, church, friends, God).

Lug like shackles homophobia's worldwide persistence.

Trudge on. It'll get better. Mother Earth will spread kinder petals.

Lose David to Stava & Tony & Jason & Michael & Brian & Jordan.

Tell no one.

Gain thirty pounds. Lose forty. Gain ten. Lose five. Damn Sikhism.

Wander through days like commandments hidden from the burning bush

Rot like a leper who other lepers call the worst leper ever.

Thrash & screech & shudder & swoon & yelp.

Tell no one.

Halftime. Primetime. Peacetime. Crunchtime.

Tell everyone.

Will 40's atheism metastasize a fuller future?

Tell everyone.

Will 50's begin and end with a broken brainstem?
Tell no one.

Will 60's veganism be the elixir to myopic bloat?
Tell everyone.

Will 70's exercise Pillars of Islam or Zen breathing?
Tell no one.

Will 80's shalom, yurt, or Confucianism?
Tell everyone.

Will 90's hedonism bolster bi-partisan liberalism?
Tell no one.

Turn 100.
Become a polytheist-egalitarian-universalist.
Tell everyone.

Turn 105.
Tell it on the mountain. So there.

BROTHERS AT THE WADENA INDOOR POOL WITH A DIVING BOARD

The neighbor Heely girls were going.
Fact. We could go, too—just round up
the dough in fifteen minutes. Tick-tock.

We raced barefoot, shifting a wake of
driveway debris from their door to ours.

I was tired of drawing mansions on a hill.
You were tired of playing a yes-sire butler.
Boyhood dryness needs summer wetness.

Male counterparts to the Heely chicks, all
of us hiding in our eyes the welts on our skin.

Their father smacked them even harder.
Their mother disappeared for weeks.
Their flower bed bred thistles & beer cans.

But they had the admission fee. We didn't.
They had an Uncle Les to drive. We didn't.

They had polka-dot beach towels. We didn't.
Hurry it up, pussies. We ain't waiting all day.
We foraged the house for a dollar-fifty fee.

I stole ninety-five cents from mom's coat pocket.
You unearthed a quarter from beneath a rug.

I recovered a dime from behind the toilet. You lifted
a dime from the bottom of the trashcan. Not enough.

Then. Ah. We dove for the nickel propping

up the kitchen table. It wobbled and tipped.
We laughed so hard. We almost missed the ride.

I wish we had. Life might be different. Somehow.

I confiscated two pennies from father's loafers.
You extracted three pennies from a sock drawer.

How little we wanted back then. Not even
two dollars. Evenness, we'd learn as men,
was not our strength, betraying us even at birth.

Our weekly allowance was the space between
parental fighting—a small gap between a large

gully of hate that always ended in it.
That's it. I've had it. Shut it. Forget it. Fuck it.
We knew who we were—the byproducts of it.

The Heely hags sang and drummed the
dashboard. Uncle Les told a joke about a fag,

a priest, a bar, & a one-legged whore named
Israel Vatican. It was funny. I think. We laughed.
I think. I was distraught. I think. Were you?

It's three dollars now. You don't have enough.
Don't look at us. We barely got it ourselves.

We sat on the sidewalk, beggars without
a cup, a sign, a clue. 2 hours felt like 4½.

You guys look homeless. Let's go, doofuses.

The Heely bitches wrung chlorine
from their bangs & bragged about
backstrokes & summersaults & air

guitar & lifeguard cuties & chocolate
pudding & cheesy bacon nacho fries.

Uncle Les parked in the back of XXX.
Life's an unfair cluster-fuck boys.
Best you learn that now.

ONE THING IS NOT LIKE THE OTHER

At 9am, I arrive

>carrying my 1,200-mile-away unrighteous gayness,
>dressed in Carolina Herrera & Hugo Boss,
>wanting acceptance influenced by love,

& am met at the front door & pointed to the kitchen table

>by my father's criticism of another unprofessional
>haircut, underemployment, & good lord
>son, can't you see God's frown upon your weight,

now come lift & haul two, forty-pound salt-pellet water-softener bags

>into the bedroom & then go in the living room
>and ask Jesus hanging above the couch about
>his repulsion with world-approving rebellion.

At 9:15am, pastor arrives

>carrying his 10-minute-away righteous straightness,
>dressed in checkered dungarees & cowboy boots,
>wanting acceptance influenced by love,

& is met at the front door & pointed to the living room couch

>by my father's Praise the Lord, look who shows up doing
>so well, great leader of the Cornerstone flock, & good
>lord son, can't you see God's smile upon your height,

now go rest & relax on this gloriously, bountiful day & flourish

in knowing Jesus's completion sees, consents,
and loves your world-denying rebellion.

THIRD SUNDAY IN JUNE

No one said Happy Father's Day. I wanted someone to say it. A child or two (or three) bringing from behind their back a wrapped gift box with a 'World's Best Dad' greeting card. A handmade coupon licensure promising free hugs, breakfast in bed, and household-chore-helper-hands ready to be activated at my right, leisure, and discretion. Arms wrapped like warm noodles around my neck. Legs buckled like a snug belt around my waist. Lips singing Happy Father's Day, Daddy, we love you so so so so so so much, shouldering the spirt of my tome-green eyes and north-steer nose and den-fort playfulness and togetherness-matters at a dining room table stippled with savor-lush comestibles where I raise a fruity-flute-drink named after me—Raderson-McDaderson—and I toast, "My dearest ones, my scented lot, my beads of aspiration, my loops of joy, my headaches of puzzlement, my elasticity of heart's sinewy chords." But I should not be so blessed, denied of fatherhood by hardwire statistics unable to partake in majority-male arousal, pursuit, and climax, neither capable of penetrating a fertile hole of expansion nor unleashing with exactitude the swimmers necessary to produce, nurture, and love a child or two (or three) lucky enough to have in the world a man, a dad, a victor, a drink, an illusion, like me.

MAN, I FEEL LIKE A WOMAN

We tossed your boobs across
the fleece coverlet waterbed
while you sun-gorged in the

backyard, our ten and six
year brotherhood bonding

over gushy-gooey-lady-
globs for a winning touchdown

as penury puberty kept us from
a football or a retractable stadium

chanting like jerks the victory
song of your silicone mastectomy

sagging from crush on the dresser
beside eyelashes and pantyhose

and now as a man I wonder
why you didn't hide them

with embarrassment of
lesser womanhood, reduced
to level-chested boydom

like us, your stemmed sprouts,
unaware in our folly how

boobs would come to shape

my deficiency of interest and
his inability to pick the right two

and your story of self-separation
entombed now in a coffin of roses
I cannot smell. Or subtract. Or release.

ANYONE BUT JESUS, WHO KEPT THEM SO FAR AWAY

An alcoholic tucked me in bed at night.
A workaholic purchased a matching gray
suit for bring-your-kid-to-work-day.
A pauper helped me memorize orbs
          and stars and craters and cosmic wreckage.
An despot scrawled a birthday card.
An embezzler sang to me Mother Goose rhymes.
A misogynist drove me to the coastline
          with the hardtop down.
A bigot laughed at my dumb puns.
A terrorist baked me chocolate chip cookies.
A racist explained Dendrochronolgy.
A convict framed elementary paintings.
A xenophobe let me win at Clue and Pictionary.
A charlatan took me bowling.
A miscreant whispered leprechaun legends.
A demagogue taught me pampootie ancestries.
An elitist showed me how to wallpaper.
A sadist commended my tennis match.
A rapist instructed me how to shave.
An autocrat skipped with me to the mailbox.
A cannibal tied my shoe laces and ascots.
A sexist arm-flailed on scads of rollercoasters.
A cat-kicker praised my grass-mowing enterprise.
A freebooter texted Sup, Buddy. You Rock.
A know-it-all assisted in amassing a hardcover
dossier of books about loyalty.
An anti-Semite cheered in the front row at
every high school auditorium and college
concerto and township Fauvism movements.

A manipulator rode motorcross in conical dunes.
A whale slayer made me BLT sandwiches.
A creep asked about my day and told
me about theirs.
A repressor read me Twain, De Pizan, & Proulx.
A dogmatist called me best friend.
An alien visited my saddest day &
eased the shades & cupped the tea
& staffed the boat & muttered,

> "I am here, dear son, to lull your
> organ pains with reanimate ovations."

BATTLESHIP

THE BRASS RAIL

I couldn't find you, lost in the glaze
of bar-fun amusement, gone for the span

of a quick piss, taunting you to weave
ones into the tinsel-chested go-go

boys' meat-thongs shading the stage
—not your thing: not mine: not really—

Why did we choose this bar?
Two-for-one cosmos, that's right.

Sorry-so-sorrying my way through hair
gel and abs, drawn to the entranceway by

your highbrow shoulders standing tall
outside without a jacket in Minnesota

chill, snowflakes flouncing the air
before nesting in your toupee—yeah, I knew—

I stood behind, wanting to spider-crawl
my fingertips across your ribcage,

wanting you to not bristle, or interrupt
the natter your upturned head was

transfixed by the skyline. Yes, at first,
softness respected the terms of privacy.

I knew I could only shelter you warm to a point.
The rest was going to be for you to do.

You walked past without murmuring hey-love or
hi-you or lets-go-in. And a degree of frostnip

gripped my throat, bearings, outlook, roots.
Frozen men, I'd learn in phases, do not thaw.

I followed your icecap to the table, stuck
to the twigs pulling inside the storm—wondering,

is snowfall merely a piece of a secret spinning around,
searching to be found, or is it the description of totality?

"You have Rudolph nose," you said.
"And you're ears are beeping."

I sat motionless, inhaling yet another daily
draining of warmth taking on bitter wind.

SLACKING ON GROUNDWORK

Stop spraying PAM onto non-stick pans.
Adding a stick of butter to a bowl of mixed
vegetables defeats the fat-free rationale.
It's my turn to mill fresh pepper and squirt
       lime juice on the tilapia.
One load of laundry: one cup of laundry detergent.
Pizza boxes and water bottles go in the recycle bin.
A flat sheet covers a fitted sheet. Always.
Pick up the vase, dust the table, set
down the vase, and continue until the
house is dust-free.
Turn down the TV volume. No, that's too low. Turn it up.
Spatulas go on the top rack of the dishwasher.
How can you not see the difference between a
       40-watt and 100-watt lightbulb?
Taking a magazine from the bathroom and
       placing it on the downstairs coffee
       table is not home renovation.
Don't you dare spit in the kitchen sink, you skrungy snit.
Warm water and Dial soap does not make window cleaner.
It's spelled AJAX. KEURIG. ORGANIC VALUE-SIZE
STREAK-FREE HARD-SURFACE STONE-DISINFECTANT.
       ALDI. MOP. JESUS. FUCK.
Watering the Ficus beside the TV isn't
       going to make it real or cause it to grow.
How big does the mouth of a trashcan have to be
to catch a Q-tip?
The exercise bike is not a clothes hamper or a hat rack
It's pronounced ARM-WHA, not ARM-OR, not hutch.
A Kleenex is not a paper towel and a paper towel

is not a washcloth.
Grass thrives when the sprinkler system is turned on.
Exchanging one dead battery for another dead battery
        does not resuscitate remote control
        unresponsiveness.
How I am supposed to trust your fidelity
        when you change the password on
        your phone innumerable times a day.

We never argued such themes.
Nor did we defend such positions.
Perhaps we should have.

SOME TRUTHS DO NOT SET US FREE

I bring a Wednesday hump-frump
to the Dunn Bros. caffeine

fanny-bumper on 26th Street, order a
hot hazelnut espresso with an extra

shot. Make it two. No, three. Okay, four.
Rococo cushions infused with eye-candy hunks

who prattle alongside an automaton-bean-
crunch-machine that's always turned on.

It's Lavender days, a mag for us
gays, The Wedding Issue, page 34—

Johnnie and Trent united at last as
fellow and blast—lucky-ass twinks—

page 35 and 36 elevating daydreams
to heartstrings, though I am in doubt.

Page 37 drags me to the depth of two
bowties—YOU GAVE HIM YOUR NAME—

11 photographs by Jenny Inc!
4 lips kissing beneath my willow tree.

3 orchid bundles centering my picnic table.
2 matching rings slicing as 1 my Pink

Champagne cake from The Salty Tart.
Faces I once fancied were smiling for us.

Piled on gifts tied with unifying ribbons
and bows keep me from looking away.

From finding disengagement. From flying on & off
the roundabout crossroads gone dark at the very end.

TEXT MESSAGE ANALYSIS

250 characters on your
10-inch smartphone

flash the strides
in your trident tongue

the slurs you
mangle into memoir

the array of your
amanuensis sniffles

and rough-weathered spurs
heckling my gale-slashed sails

cordoning an unorthodox
alliance with oust from the abundance

of your plump thumbs & bleak
judgments forging triggers within

the stab & slice of your
on-screen swordsmanship.

MOMENTOUS

I am no one's shrine.
Neither god nor goddess.
No one's temple or prayer.
Nor plea. Nor tempter.

Nor temptress. No one's lust.
No one's full-size. Or king-size.
Or queen-size. No reign at all.
Nor rule. Nor kingdom.

No one's galaxy.
Neither star nor starlet.
No one's cosmos or ether.
Nor constellation. Nor borealis.

Nor borealis-2. No one's milky.
No one's way. Or Mercury.
Or Mars. No Saturn at all.
Nor Uranus. Nor Pluto.

No one's fusion.
Neither chrome nor chromium.
No one's concept or genre.
Nor trove. Nor acclaim.

Nor acclimation. No one's aero.
No one's dynamic. Or leather.
Or leatherette. No speed at all.
Nor pace. Nor traction.

No one's tulip.
Neither bulb nor bulbous.
No one's perennial or show.
Nor showmanship. Nor seed.

Nor seedling. No one's reddish.
No one's bluish. Or winter.
Or summer. No season at all.
Nor spring. Nor fall.

No one's table.
Neither knobby nor knotty.
No one's slab or stone.
Nor stoned. Nor stupor.

Nor stupendous. No one's birch.
No one's pine. Or elm.
Or oak. No rings at all.
Nor record. Nor data.

No one's stream.
Neither carp nor carpe diem.
No one's river or bay.
Nor cove. Nor tributary.

Nor trickle. No one's constant.
No one's flow. Or drift.
Or ocean. No current at all.
Nor tide. Nor surge.

I am no one's no one.
Today.

WRAPPED IN DRAPERY SOMNOLENCE

You were a bolt of
cashmere engraving the ledge.

I was a slip of satin
halving the ridge.

We were an armature of
airdura masking the bluff.

ROLEX'S NEW KING

Thin times flat a wristwatch is key,
links a steel band with an oyster sea,
a master's gift from me to me,
its face as round as time proceeds.

Split days clang on though we do not,
like ruminations Timex forgot,
like losing every fight I fought
to prove my worth without a spot

or right of mine to cash and coin
as courts devoid the interjoin
of man on man does not eloign
with customary tenderloin.

Taxes are due by robotic shake,
demanding stocks I do not make,
no trade, no bread, no fems, no fake,
might Rolex be pawn for a bill's outbreak?

We meet at Perkins where I deal in whole,
all sales are final like your Mexican mole.
One-third of its price and that's when I know
you steal and barter and minefield my soul.

I curb every debt and am walking high-lighter,
when you wear it at work, do you feel brighter?
A friend, a friend said, amidst an all-nighter
would have given me more, had I been an outsider.

I throb and I snip in the coup of this sting,
how tick is to tock as sprung is to spring.
And I cannot forget how curtly you sing
the song of sedition as Rolex's new king.

CITIZENSHIP

LAUGHING CLASS USA, THOUGH NOT AS MUCH. RIGHT?

1. TO THE CLOUDS EVERYWHERE

Prejudice soapboxes keep shrinking.
The you're-less-than-us stampede

can't feel their toes. Some of the
smear, fear, and cheer campaigns

have cut some of the chains from
some of the turnstiles while myriad

platforms are being disassembled
and reassembled for tonight's equal

rights rally. The bolted chairs of the
in-betweener's and the I-don't-like-to-

get-involved's have unmoored and are
mingling with the glitter posters, bylaw-badges,

and bumper stickers in the red light districts
still chasing a seat at humanities table to unfurl a coil of sneers.

AIDS is the new hominid elevation.
In-service is the new breaking bad.

Harmony is scripture fulfilling its purpose.
One wins. All win. Like GLAAD. Like rad.

2. MY WIFE, MAN – MAY 14, 2013 – MINNESOTA LEGALIZES SAME-SEX MARRIAGE

Eons ago, I fell for a three-story jewel, an acclivitous back yard, an older man, and myself. Neither in this particular order nor with any ease of acquisition. But they did happen. The front yard needed refurbishment. The landscape beds craved river rock. The six trees with overhanging branches required pruning. And two naughty arborvitae were blocking the living room window from viewing the street. So I paid a tree service three-hundred dollars to come dig, carry, and haul them away. I know the age of wanting to stare out the window at the street is coming, and I can't have two naughty arborvitae blocking my view.

First, I met the neighbors Benny and Donna and their chirp-nub puppy, Socrates. Benny asked if I had a wife. His name is man, I said. Benny frowned and Donna offered a right hand.

Second, I met the neighbors Scott and Katherine but not their kids, a pair of twins named Paul and Saul or Chip and Kip or some rhyme-scheme derivation. Katherine asked if I had a wife. His name is man, I said. Scott cleared his throat and Katherine giggled.

Third, I didn't meet the neighbors—Mr. and Mrs. Homophobe—lawyer-saints who lurk across the street in a white salt box with black shutters and a thick-peeling front door. No welcome to the neighborhood. No apple pie. No equally-cut brownies. No invitation to the annual summer linen party The City Journal calls a community unification project designed to empower citizens to become watchmen, partners, and friends. The lawyer-saints did not agree, averting eyes whenever I tossed a wave from the same mailbox attached to the same red,

white, and blue pole I painted every July: a proud American,
like them, I hope. Maybe they'll move. Maybe they'll change.

3. RHETORIC BY NATURE

What is the poison of me
that is no poison at all?

What is the unlawfulness
segregating my breed
again and again (and again)?

What is the hell of me that could
be such heaven if I just wasn't so me?

4. BURGEONING ACERBITY

"Homosexuals miss ecstasy."

Oh, how my parents convulsed.
"Christian, Normal, Christian.

And if you are not,
then you're no son of ours.

No faggot for us will do.

Is that how you want to live?
Is this how you want to die?"

***

But wait, there's a ringtone,
a note, a knock at the door.

"And if you are, then
you're still our son.

No faggot for us will do.

That's no way to live.
That's no way to die."

5. HALLOWEEN 2010

Two fog machines puffed eerie smoke into the concrete porch.
Add sinister music, strobe lights, and a healthy dose of yarn-
knit webbing, our house was a supernatural place to trick or
treat. My makeup and rhinestone tiara had congealed. Damn
it, if I wasn't the hottest looking groovy-afro-devil-princess
ever. Inside the door, I held an orange bowl brimming with
mini-snickers, lollipops, and multi-colored gummy bears. A
batch of pirates and fairies ran by, but no plastic sword or daz-
zle-wing-ballerina rang the doorbell. I turned off the lights.
I turned them back on. Be patient. They'll come. A clump
of Superman's, one springy-faced Nixon, and two matching
tigers skipped down the street. I grabbed the bowl and pressed
an ear against the door. No doorbell. No knock. No smell my
feet. No I want something good to eat. I opened the door—all
appeared well as hell. I restarted the music, which blared a
little loud, but so what, so did the amps, and so did I. A swarm
of teens in jeans burst down the street. "They're way too old,"
I whispered. I'm right here, I thought. No jean came to the
door: not a small one, not a tall one, nor one as big as a ball,
rejecting the fog machine and the crinkly-wrapped candy I'd
bought for them, not for me. An hour zipped by. Nothing. No
one. Nil. I brought in the speakers, turned off the smoke ma-
chine, and slammed the door. I left the lights on. Just in case.

6. ACCEPTANCE

Celebrate the gay in the gayness.
It's okay. A lot of people are doing it.

7. VERBAL EUTHANASIA

Don't say faggot, unless you're smoking a cigarette or buying
meatballs in London—or queer,
say remarkable instead—flamer,
unless you're confronting a hot corpse of incinerating gas—butt pi-
rate, unless you're friends with a Pirate whose name is Butt Pirate—
pedophile, healthy gay people, like healthy straight people,
do not molest children—unnatural,
we're some of the most eco-friendly vanguards in the world—
immorality, unless you're name-bombing Putanism—
degenerate, unless you're going blind—bull-dyke,
that's just awful—cock jockey, nobody under the age of 96
says that anymore—butt buddies,
if you must quote South Park—light in the loafers,
talk about cliché—sodomite,
okay, yes, some LGBTQI people have anal sex, call it that if you
must—homo,
unless you add sexual and say it with respect—fairy,
unless you're Tinker Bell or some other Disney character with
wings—fruit,
seriously, grow up—queen,
unless you're addressing her royal majesty, Elizabeth—
Mary/Nancy, unless those are their God given names—pansy,
really?—back door bandit,
unless someone breaks into your home via the back door and then
by all means yell, scream, do whatever it takes to get the back
door bandit out of your house. Duh.

Actually, don't say these words at all.
Say hi.
LGBTQI people respond well to hi.
Hi.

8. THANK YOU, U.S. SUPREME COURT 2015

From Main Street to Duck Dynasty,
the Earth belongs to Venus, too,
every ring, gold circle to blue air,
serves as a symbol and not as a

simulation of a marriage commitment
that isn't based on sex or those who
choose to have it with men or with women
or with less than two or with more than

five, but with love, life's longest migration
pointing us to be kind, I beseech you, for in the
end we are all the same vernacular,
hair, water, pestilence, tissue, tears,

bone, and synapse: a click and a flick:
a mug and a slug: a storehouse of
dreamers dreaming dreams of coexistence:
dais to apex saluting everyone:

the bi-tri-curious
the transfigured
the scissor sisters

the cut it straights
the reds to the violets
the grahams to the sims

the closeted marrieds
the openly besties

the wonderful gay
is the wonderful me.

let me say it again—

the wonderful gay
is the wonderful me.

SAN BERNARDINO & PARIS & TURKEY & LONDON & BELGIUM & ORLANDO & ME

I'm frightened, quivering as media-mania
news coverage touts damage and death,
reporters stalking the scene for tag-bite cash,
anchors sensationalizing viewership ratings,
perpetrator's fame scrolling across TV screens,
victims gore covering the pages of People magazine,
silent prayers filtering through Google & Twitter.
Reddit implodes while watercoolers stay relevant.
Foreign-ills become the street on which we live,
the café in which we eat, the concert in which
we sing, the mega-venue in which we cheer, the
sanctuary in which we pray, the bar in which we dance,
the planet in which we frack, the sky in which
we pollute, the heaven in which we ask God
to choose our side and bless our cause.
Now is the era of radicalized dogmas
disseminated by fanatic extremists who abrade
a love of hate so utterly encased in bullets
and banks and beheadings and brands,
murder has ruined my faith in the middle.
And the east. Crime ropes tribes and idols
to livestock and trees. And conventions.
Whoever breaks a circle destroys its link.
Al-Qaeda sounds like a children's party host.
ISIS is two helping verbs working side by side.
Fallujah rhymes with Hallelujah. Nice is nice.
Why do the names Syed and Abdullah and Omar
and Hussein threaten me more than the names
Timothy and Jeffrey and Charles and James? How
do U.S. drones in tribal lands prove nationalism?

Does military hypocrisy only apply to communists?
Is the furrow on which I drive more sacred than the
cell from which we all arrive? Is peace a pun?
Is goodwill the pen name of Platonic criticism? Is
solidarity only a vision meant for naive visionaries?
Panic has me checking my back. At the library.
Leeriness quickens my pace. At the barbershop.
Skepticism fiddles with the locks. At the stoplight.
Mistrust deviates from the plot. At the movies.
Xenophobia wrecks collaboration. At the core.
Stay away from crowds. Avoid the seven wonders.
A smoke grenade can be made in a kitchen.
A pipe dream shares history with a pipe bomb.
Every face is suspect. Sunglasses times two.
Every frown commandeers camouflage caution.
Every backpack, even polka-dots, is a tomb
for knives, guns, nooses, drugs, cuffs, bombs.
Every purse. Gym bag. Envelope.
Mailbox. Courthouse. Arby's.
Gatorade. Candy bar. Taxi.
Pill. Cell phone. Computer.
Chair. Shoe. Pocket. Cross.
Evangelist. Cleric. Door chime. Keystone.
If someone pops chewing gum, I cringe.
If someone cracks a knuckle, I wince.
If a child bawls, I gallop the other way.
If an adult cries, I cower behind a child.
Goosebumps and hair-raise are not in decline.
Most windows are not ammunition proof.
Security codes and clearances can be easily hacked.
What does WIFI really mean, really do, really say?
Civilization can absorb only so many acts of war.
Perhaps mortality's self-annihilation is what
the earth's crust has been burning for all along.

DEAR FOUNDING FATHERS

The People revere Sir Washington stout,
all six foot three with a pasty-white snout.
In Trumbull hues or as Giuseppi's muse,
he's corset tight with sash in sight to ruse
a bust, a wig, a purse, a snob, a cock.

Poor Martha's view, what can she do but see
regalia stomp and romp in nation wristed glee.
A face dressed up, a war brought down, berate
chapped lips that raze the wind abuzz with hate
for minutemen held-hands predawn the clock.

Hamilton too, and sweet Jeel-Bare, and Jack,
that gaily horde, bright Fred Baron von Clack,
who tailored the troops in marching parade
as sacrosanct bulges and laces and braids,
for boys are boys—a fact as hard as rock.

George with his dates returns each year
in epaulet worship, most fashion queer.
Dare we forget the Federalist Papers,
the Bank, the Mint, the usury capers;
our President One, our dandy in frock, our
false teeth, our well-bred, our fairytale stock.

CIRCUMLOCUTION

Do you ever think of me?
I focus on the good times.

Can you name one?
It's too hard, there's so many.

Where are you living?
Here and there until I figure things out.

Where is your mattress?
I gave it to a friend.

Which friend?
Some guy at work who needed one.

Where are you sleeping?
Actually better than I have in years.

Where do you shower?
The gym has a nice one.

You go to a gym?
Just a little one downtown.

Downtown where?
It's a pretty, dingy place.

Where are your clothes?
I'm living out of a suitcase.

Where's your suitcase?
It varies week to week.

Are you looking for a house?
Everything out there's so expensive.

You've gotta be staying somewhere.
I'm not even thinking about that right now.

You're not thinking about a place to stay?
I've got a few options but nothing's tied down.

Where are your dishes and silverware?
I boxed 'em up and donated 'em.

To who?
I don't recall anymore. Probably Savers.

Where are you eating?
I need to get to the gym more often.

Are you still driving the Lexus?
I'm definitely buying used next time.

I wish you'd tell me the truth.
I thought I was.

No, I mean, what's really going on.
Some days I have no idea.

Are you feeling okay?
I will be once I figure everything out.

I hope you'll keep me posted.
I'm just glad the weather's getting nicer.

I guess there's that.
Okay then, thanks for calling.

I miss you.

OLD MEN WHEREABOUTS

Like forever the two men sit in the porch on matching
green recliners facing each other like reflective mirrors.

The one man sips Earl Gray tea and writes poetry.
The other man smokes a pipe and reads the newspaper.

At 8:30pm, hand in hand, they go upstairs to bed.
Standard fare since retirement, almost twenty years ago next May.

The one man enjoys the quiet but misses the younger days of laughter.
The other man enjoys the quiet but misses the younger days of sex.

"Would you like to hear my latest poem?" the one man asks the other
man.
"Course," the other man says, smoking a pipe. "Ready whenever you
are."

The one man lifts with arthritic fingers the sheet of paper.
"Just a few lines about who we once were and who've we've become."

The other man smiles. "Short and sweet. Just like I like 'em."
"You'll tell me if it's good when I'm finished, yeah?"

"I always do."
"Like forever," the one man begins.

"The two men sit in the porch on matching green
recliners facing each other like reflective mirrors."

He pauses and looks up. "You like it?"

"Go on. I know there's more."
"What do you think of it so far?"

"Nice introduction. I can really see the setting."

"Splendid." He continues the poem, an ode,
finishing out of breath as the other man's pipe tips

and burns the edges of the newspaper.

He too is out of breath, exiting with the
same inferno by which he entered.

THE TWO STALL BATHROOM IN NORDSTROM'S BASEMENT

You want to know about my favorite public restroom, don't you?
Why I drive twenty-nine miles one way to get there.
How I shirk-work and race-pace and park-shark and so-lo.
Hint one: Lust and its Catch-and-Release Routine.

You want to know about my stall virgule, don't you?
Why I sit on a toilet seat for an hour, often two.
How I wait-gait and play-sway and grow-show and ear-steer.
Hint two: Touch of the Here-and-Now Nirvana.

You want to know about the scent I crave, don't you?
Why I interface the partition to inhale male ripeness.
How I sniff-wiff and snap-trap and stretch-fetch and stroke-poke.
Hint three: Linkage to a Beg-And-Borrow Advertisement.

You want to know about my evolution of readiness, don't you?
Why I risk being caught for the few minutes of being caught.
How I knee-agree and hand-stand and feet-greet and finger-linger.
Hint four: Regularity of a Top-to-Bottom Lonesomeness.

You want to know about my tile-floor addiction, don't you?
Why I slide a prick and drill with willpower greed.
How I pitch-rich and bite-right and kiss-piss and strum-cum.
Hint five: Magnetism of the No-Strings-Attached Sex.

You want to know about my blowout undoing, don't you?
Why I ask for things no one gives or takes or shares or repairs.
How I lone-alone and blame-defame and stress-less and gait-late.
Hint six: Weariness of Restroom Anonymity.

You want to know about my afterward unwinding, don't you?
Why I curse traffic jams and little children singing in car seats.
How I sigh-dry and door-floor and slink-drink and bed-tread.
Hint seven: Chagrin of Unsatisfying Repetition.

You want to know about my promise to not go again, don't you?
Why I make another round of inconsequential vows.
How I stay-away and snatch-latch and porn-scorn and blight-sight.
Hint eight: Deception of Seeker Changeability.

You want to know about my raging mind-fuck, don't you?
Why I fight an arcane root stymied by castigation.
How I frantic-antic and twist-list and file-nubile and haul-pall.
Hint nine: Pressure from Glandular Fixation to Recidivism.

You want to know about my self-acceptance, don't you?
Why I outta be so ashamed you can't believe your eyes.
How I throw-glow and dim-rim and dearth-worth and my-oh-my.
Hint ten: Prince to the Outright Kingdom of a Beloved Pastime.

GAY MEN'S UNCOUPLING GROUP

Obsessed with cynicism.
The room doesn't even have a number.

Welcome ya'll—

Turf carpeting.
Fluorescent lava lamps.

Just remember—

staying means living
and leaving means dying
and it's easier to plug
a nose than a heart.

So—

I sit on the verge of a light-brown couch
and cross my arms, hands, and legs
as men appear: two slender, three silver
daddies, a black-belt karate uniform,
a red-drab-slump face, four or five
on-point buzz cuts, and a sad fag (that's me),
plus six or seven other dudes missing the
components of interesting construction.

Perhaps—

They come seeking on-point buzz cuts.
They come seeking uniformity.

They come seeking a silver daddy.
They come seeking a sad fag.

Relax—

Let Jerry, the bolo-tie-bear-moderator, detail
the evening rules painted in black on a dull
white divider: check-in, respect, listen, feedback,
support, check-out, be well, be safe,
be kind, be yourself, be kind to yourself.

It's time to unveil, ya'll. Why not give it away—

Hmm—

Jeff hates a maniacal, bipolar ex-lover
who owes him five-hundred dollars
and Landon wants a hot husband who
can stay on track and Barry and his
ten-year old daughter are moving out
of his third partner's apartment for
a third time and Tim feels leery confronting
his father about replacing expired fishing
boat tabs and Joshua ran stairs for
five minutes yesterday and Kevin
believes same–sex marriage is conforming
by way of exhonerating past oppressors
who shouldn't get a free pass just because
equality is the new social hispter
and Trevor is currently exploring the
ranks of match dot com and Renslow
took a three-hour nap in a sauna today
and Benji is choosing pain over suicide
and I'm just a sad fag striving to over-

haul a rusted, busted-up engine.

Perhaps—

I've come seeking a three-hour nap.
I've come seeking a free pass.
I've come seeking a fishing boat.
I've come seeking a maniacal, bipolar ex-lover.

Thanks for sharing, ya'll—

Benji asks about my engine metaphor.
Trevor asks if I work and where do I live.
Landon asks who are you, really?
Jerry asks what I hope to gain or lose.

It's simple—

coming means advancing
and returning means surviving
and it's easier to grieve when
someone else is listening.

CENSORSHIP

SELF-AWARENESS IS A SKILL
OF A VERY SPECIAL KIND

I've come to enter daily outings without you
as a question, carrying the pressure of its mark:

Who am I now in this space?

I have not heard back from our preferred
Starbucks, Target, Kowalski's, Macy's,

BODYSTEP 12, mailbox number 10,
Carmike theatre 8, home by 6, Jacuzzi on 4,

boxed-hoagies for 2, savings at 0. Whether
I am greater than these mundanities

or smaller than their smallest parts
is a scale of conjecture, as I am deaf

to the language of my own estimation.

Yet I continue to wield breakthroughs
compass with the task of finding a-me-

spot that might dispel the myth that one is
a lesser, overcast existence than two

and that I, pupil and iris, have not fallen
so far behind. I land in Paradise Park—

the newspaper headlines its edifice,
radiance, modernism, novelty, and bustle—

and sit on a bench encircling a Blue Beech
Tree shading an indoor waterfall spilling

top-heavy secrets into a pond richer with
wishes than pennies, pebbles, and minnows.

I wonder how many, if any, have come true.

Perhaps the value of a wish is as much about
the throw as it is dreaming of purer waters—

grant it autonomy and let it find its own heads or tails.

I am not among the coins in the pond, neither
glinting copper nor illustrious gold, and the only

silver I catch ripples against side-hair reflection.
I am not a blazing ray from the track lighting nor

a groove coating the slippery floor. I am not a screw
bolting the maritime stools, nor do I

spot my thin-grin in the fifty-five
mural photos of resident townsfolk.

That would take a miracle.

Like not flipping through photo albums you
didn't want, funny-man portraits I cut and pasted

of farmyard muscle, calculus zoos, pumpkin fritters,
popsicle wizards, and eventide-flicker-lick eyelashes.

You are everywhere, and nowhere, all at once.

Doing a terrific job of doing nothing more than
circumscribing me to the mist of rewound evaporation.

I stare at the Park's ceiling, marvel at a
row of steely trusses upholding the roof,

count forty-four windows curating the
sunlight augmenting a heap of corrugated ferns

climbing over the walls—additional proof that
grounded things will try to escape their confines.

I am glad to not be in the recycle, compost,
or trash bins. Nor am I hanging on any hanger

among the many other hangers. The information
kiosk shares none of my irrelevance and Miss Angelina's

Deli smells only of wonder woman ice cream and
strawberry shortcake and pecan puff lady fingers.

I am not in the moan of the Coca-Cola machine
nor in the syrupy jizz dripping from the nozzle.

I am neither the coolness flowing from the
vents nor the stability of the iron handrails.

Then I see it, spiraling the air, brushing the
concrete, a Ficus Alii leaf, with its uneven lines

and aging blemishes and a chunk of its heart is missing

from the middle of its spine. It's lucky I saved it.
Now no one can step on it or kick it out of the way.

A Ficus Alii leaf, in this space is who I am without you.

But wait, who is that exquisite man eyeing my Ficus
Alii leaf, tittering at my stare, standing up to my awareness,

waving me to follow his invitation—one-
step-two-step—into the bathroom to pull

it all down and bring it all out and kneel
and suck and fasten and tuck because

action like reaction reveals the amplitude
of who I am with or without you, known not

by what I took but by what I left, a blot of
sticky scum marring the earth, just as you said.

ORPHAN DOGS

After our final PRIDE, we (you, me and a yappy terrier named
Bentley) unleashed from the SexWorld bag onto the bedspread
the sum of PRIDE'S tchotchke loot: condoms and frisbees and
Blow Pops and two lime-green New Testament Gideon Bibles
from a horde of neckties who still believe God can change
queer to clear. Hissing at the neckties, Bentley licking the loot,
we were almost over it. It's tragic, how quickly gay men with
little dogs can move on. I gave the bag one last jiggle. A business
card from the Humane Society of Minneapolis fell to the floor.
"You're not tchotchke loot anymore," you told Bentley. The
rain came. We'd heard it was coming. I sat beside you on the
carpet and passed between us the business card, Bentley, and a
cigarette, taking from each the design for which it was made:
matted cages littered with whatnot burning for home.

During our final PRIDE, we (you, me and thousands more free)
roamed the white tent grid in a park with a playground for
urbanite children missing the air of a swing, the rush of a slide,
the grasp of a monkey bar, the queers of a sideshow. I tied to
our wrists strings faithful to a bunch of We-R-Family balloons.
I mummified our bare chests with errant tye-dye streamers
from the YMCA carnival float. I yelled at the Gideons, "We're
not tchotchke loot but we'll take your lime-green Bibles any-
way." I snapped a picture of us in front of the Humane Society
of Minneapolis booth, cuddling a yappy terrier named Corky
you renamed Bentley, and posted it on Facebook—271 likes:
69 comments: 6 shares in ten minutes. You'd think we were
happy. You'd think we loved PRIDE. You'd think Bentley the
luckiest terrier in Minnesota. You'd think we were forecasting
the future.

Before our final PRIDE, we (just you and me), scrambled eggs in silence, showered alone, argued procession thoroughfares, disputed parking fees, and itemized each other's shortcomings—I'm surprised we arrived anywhere intact. A billboard sign on Highway 94 got us talking. HAPPY PRIDE FROM THE HUMANE SOCIETY OF MINNEAPOLIS: a yappy terrier plastered on both sides. "I wonder why there's always so many dogs at PRIDE in need of adoption," I said. "That's easy," you replied, without pause. "If orphan gays in orphan days can save orphan dogs from orphan ways, then orphan dogs in orphan ways can save orphan days from orphan gays, who've been compared for far too long as tchotchke loot."

WATER FOUNTAIN MEN

burbling sweat
drip-drops
on bare knees
& compression
short-shorts &
mesh-tennies
spinning the cycle
number 10 of 12
stationary greys
planted firmly
on speckle terrazzo
neither motto nor mantra
but a vascular process
of calorie shred
that's more or less
a daylight ritual
I cannot quit
hamstring stretching
as butt reduction
brings waist to a waist
risen by Snickers
and Goobers & You
I'm still craving
badly
seventeen minutes to go,
come on sport,
work off the hunger,
when two power belts ransack
the water fountain &
guard each other's universe:

lap it up—
lick it up—
laugh it up—
    fondness & kinship
galvanize my endorphins
    with a rampage refrain—
        might there…
        somewhere…
        out there…
be a water fountain man
    to guard over my universe, too.

FLAIR

The size of an orgasm,
a FUN METER button

you gave as wearable
proof that I rate somewhere

between the black pointer's
pendulum tottering minimum blue

and medium yellow and maximum
red, tipping high-red the day you

pinned to my chest every
tee-hee, handspring,

green light, flavor, and jolt.
There's no one cuter. Or funnier. Or prouder.

So I wore out the red for you,
leaving yellow to the mediocre,

the status quo, the fickle, the needy;
leaving blue to the duds, the desolate,

the dismayed, the seriously out-of-sync;
leaving two years later on a Thursday

breeze without a choice, or a proposal,
setting the button tipping low-blue

on a chipped desk in a rented room from
a General Manager at Buick who asked

last week while caulking the egresses
why I never wear it anymore and will it

ever turn red again and does it
prick me if I whisper your name.

HEAR NO EVIL, SPEAK NO EVIL

You're about to hear short words
of which you need to repeat back,
the audiologist says, standing above

me as I complain of hearing loss:
buzzing, popping, jabbing knife
pain—sometimes in my ears. The

rubber chair imbues sciatic soreness.
I'm gonna leave and shut the door.

Stay seated and follow the prompts.
I am not fond of bossy, older women.
It'll be over with before you even know it.

A male voice, half-android, half-phone
sleaze says through the earphones,
"Say the word boat." I cannot speak.

Our second date rented a boat from
which we swam, kissed, drank Stewart's,
sang McGraw, and danced nighttime Bebop.

"Say the word shout." No. Our last day
at Guider Drive entrapped us within
violent expletives throwing punches.

I'm having trouble hearing you.

"Say the word limb." Our first hug

liberated every compartment in my body from
years of blockade self-deprecation.

You need to speak up.

"Say the word tough." Our wounded
exteriors molded by societal diehards
dehumanizing our social currency.

Are you hearing the words?

"Say the word choice." Truth
is, we didn't have one, neither
in the springtide nor in the fall.

Do you want me to start over?

"Say the word page." Our messy
chapters written in weak sentences
by character-assassination plots.

Do you want me to come in there?

"Say the word week." Our saddest
homophone and stingiest noun and
cruelest verb and nastiest adjective.

Do you need a break?

"Say the word burn." Every blister
and bump and scorch and singe and
blotch and peel and crumble and ash.

Do you need a drink of water?

"Say the word love." I stand.
"Say the word over." I wipe my cheekbones.
"Say the word grief." I set the earphones on the floor.

Why didn't you repeat the words?
she criticizes me for leaving
things exactly as I found them.

ONE TEENSY-WEENSY FAVOR

May I come like morning dew and
blanket your skyscraper newness

and saturate with kisses dimple
imprints and parry with balm

every visceral pockmark refracting
mind-echoes from heart-pangs

pulling from the lies we needn't
rant every truth we mustn't decry

THANKSGIVING DAY PARADE

Do-do-do-do: your happy kitchen tune
in cookery mode, turning a family recipe

into a meal for two, *for me and you,*
you say, mister hip-wiggler, mister no-rhythm,

mister elbow-cluck, mister no-coordination,
mister moonwalker, mister no-popstar-moves.

       You're no Ricky Martin.

Taste this. You bring to my lips a steaming
spoonful of cranberry relish. Which I refuse.

A first sign of sabotage. A second rate dis. And dish.
A third, no a fourth cup of scalding nullification.

       You're no Bobby Flay.

Do-do-do. Shorter this time. Quieter, too.
No wiggle. No elbow. No hips. No really.

Not hungry. Eat without me. My tenement bedroom
tune eviscerating what I can't enjoy.

       You're no Father Time.

Knock. Knock. Knock. Dinner's ready.
Not hungry. Eat without me.

But I worked so hard. I made all your favs.
Not hungry. Eat without me.

You're no Captain Hook.

How dare you take pleasure in seasoning?
How dare you bake candies I can only taste sour?
How dare you try to sweeten holiday childhood pain?

You're no Charlie Brown.

I refute turkey broiled with pleasure.
I snub tables spread with matching sets.
I despoil affection poised by consistency lips.

You're no better than me.

We both know (so well) (done)
I'll materialize hours later
and pick at things until it all falls apart—
until there's absolutely nothing left—

You're no Roast Beast.

SEQUENTIALLY OFF LIMITS

rise to sniff alarm trill decoding your dreams
chase your foot bark rousing the master bathroom

leap into Pima cotton threads restoring your towel
dance on the lightbulb flexing your drowse

hide between razor blades licking your nicks
coat the Listerine cap tickling your palm

hop across fingerprints squeezing your tweezer
squat in the cologne nozzle lusting your neck

drop into molar wiggle your tongue teases clean
climb over hairbrush dowels combing your steppe

cling to jawline age spots decomposing your luminosity
whuffle exhaust fan fumes embossing your oxygenation

sit in the mirror crack you talked of replacing
wait atop a floss pick you tossed aside and forgot

OWNERSHIP

LOOK

I've screamed
accusations
at depression: *waste*
                  victim
                  coward
                  failed experimentation

and I can concede with   tear-screen
documentation   and ripcord
                    memorization

      that it is a scalpel dropping
its tip with pinpoint precision

into the   center   of my heart

to bleed out   what's
already   blood-dry.

YOUR DRESSER

In the top drawer
sit a pair of socks
with a wee hole
in the middle toe.
In the second drawer
sit five pair of red
briefs in a baggie
with a pink receipt.
In the third drawer
sit four Levi blue
jeans with a rip in
the right kneecap.
In the fourth drawer
sit three pair of tan
dress shoes in dire
need of a trashcan.
In the fifth drawer sit
two wool-puff sweaters
expecting your shoulders.
In the sixth drawer sit nine
rolls of film of date nights,
day trips, Maui, and Ireland
awaiting a yellow eviction slip.

HEART MONITOR

Fingertip a popper-top wrist-vein.
Ninety-nine beats per minute.

Sorry for overworking you.

Pledge of allegiance hand shields
the breastplate, moves stethoscope

epidermis across fatigue, strain,
tenderness, & meltdown.

Sorry for subverting you.

Why can't I transmit you better?
Why am I always so agony-rushed?

I want for you salve happiness.
It takes muscle to grow.

How can I drop you off at loss &
let you tremble in its darkness?

I want for you tonic sunshine.
It takes courage to glow.

Sorry for hiding you.

Such a fickle host. I expose you
to anesthetized war zones

of mayhem. Test your capacity
for regurgitated unrest.

Twist your fisted fibre. Condemn your
lust for blood. Shame your orientation.

Push you to run faster. Demean your pace.
Promise rejuvenation. Ignore reality pleas.

Leave you to knock knock (knock) against
the sternum—is anyone home? can

anyone hear me? does anyone care
if I bruise, break, or bust?—which is why

I pray to the lungs of the next host,
the anti-me, the elixir-me, the

spark-star team player who'll
turn every fault line tribulation

into equilibrium wonderment.
Amen. Sorry for failing you.

VACATION RE-VISITATION

An email advertisement from The Preserve Company
in Prince Edward Island thirty-two months later still

scrapes my wishbone, rearranges my outline,
trips me backward in the discomfort of knowing

this harbor-place, with its torches, inventions,
and observation deck couldn't parce the fragments

of our blight, despite the magic stroll from
the restaurant to the Garden of Hope holding

hands in the open among the busy bees of the
meadow, my heart teeming with belonging,

your smile educating springtime blossoms, our
arms swinging up and back like measured men

co-opting reassurance with parity at dinner,
but only after a long steam-physique

deluge and a few high-five oaths to intersect
harder this round, tucking at dusk into suitcases

six, twelve-ounce jars of raspberry-champagne jelly
for the happier, wiser breakfasts at home in a

state where the loons govern the lakes,
whispering we're so (not) good at bedtime beneath

Anne Shirley's resplendent Canadian moon
setting on without us to shine on wiser shores.

MAY 29

I forgive you
for every crisscross serration
stitched into my mass
by pricking needlepoint

inscribing an amalgam
of borderless grafts and
pilloried nicks and din rifts
and writ breaches and mortar faults

infecting my bloodstream
with filament shrapnel
tightening my senses
by stringing my thoughts

to unevenness
to disproportion
to one-sidedness
to inconsistency

but through time's transfusing
stages I have come to catharsis,
absolving every broken heartbeat
with every broken bone

and I hope through time's transfusing
stages you have come to catharsis
and have forgiven every crisscross
serration I stitched into you.

WE ALL REACH

deterioration

    says a shrinking oak leaf
    severed from its branch.

displacement

    says a fray-winged jaybird
    culled from its flock.

disillusionment

    says a wilting-yellow mimulus
    transplanted from its root.

desertion

    says a tainted memory collector
    faded from its photograph.

ANOMALOUS

Weird walking the mall with you, as
friends, if that's who we are, you never say.

Odd maintaining self-sufficiencies,
you used to maintain mine, funny pretending

our bodies haven't consumed each other's
cartilage, nerves, hallucinations, and potions.

Bizarre ordering for one at Panda Express,
we used to piece-meal tips, keeping now to the bite

of my own basket, yearning to feed
native lips finger-licking aftertastes.

Strange trying on clothes in separate
dressing rooms, wishing the well-lit mirror

could reconvene our nakedness
and let me sketch once again

monogram flesh I have not stopped signing.
Eerie saying goodbye without an embrace,

peculiar driving to opposite sides of the city, as
friends, if that's who we are, you never say.

VERTICAL TRACES OF HORIZONTAL MUTENESS

I'd cannibalize one opinion

Concerning our history(onics)
After fog-squalid-circuits-estranged,
Now that I've absorbed the earthquake,
Now that I've permitted the numbing side effect
Of carrying forward a past without definition: hazed
Theories like ghosts I can outline but cannot suffuse,

Burrowing teardrops into fossilized gaps of
Erasure, extemporization, eugenics even, but

You must retain one assessment,
One loophole, one apologia, one social skill
Underneath the layers of ad-hominem and austerity and Asperger's
Rubric, one bit of dialect we shared like air for a decade-plus, so

How can I convince you of my need to not write my own
Explanation of our testimony—I am capable of this—
          but to unleash your
Reminiscence—you are capable of this—because if you can throw it
Out there, maybe I can cease cross-examining the slow, uniform pitch
          of it all.

I HURT

          like an

enemy who whispers friendship with
hushed glyphs of glut destabilization.

I can relieve numbness with destruction.
I can lift lowness higher by gashing you up.

I can create chaos astonishment in minutes,
what took God in heaven seven days.

I can fill fracas distortion with blind
eyes and seal it with deaf eardrums.

I can manipulate digits to
help cleanse filth from your palette.

I can alleviate the tummy-ache,
the tooth-ache, the head-ache, the

body-ache of liquidating a father who
calls you less and hangs up whenever

you ask for more and siblings who never
call and only pick up to say how-now-

brown-cow and friends who congratulate
your parody prance of perfection and

strangers who need you to be fine when

they ask, how are you doing, I trust you're fine.

Skinny jeans is the populace measurement
success uses to conquer scope and ruler.

Rib and spine definition poke a new
notch in the narrowing belt of backbone.

Chipmunk cheeks, double chin, love
handles, and quadriceps all sound fat.

There's nothing light about cellulite.
There's nothing lax about laxatives.

What goes in must come out.
Norm since the serpent-slither of mankind.

Difference is power expunging weakness.
I can strip combustion from disorder until only

the eradication of well-being remains.

I can run you down because I know
numbers reflect brainwave propulsion.

I can reach the phantoms bullying the
comparisons lining your blackouts.

I can muzzle through starvation every
falsehood hunger foments as honesty.

There's nothing more filling than emptiness.
There's nothing more transparent than a skeleton.

I can make you prized. I can fix the errors.
I am guardian. I am transporter. I am an emergency

exit sign glistening above a revolving door.
Give yourself over to me. Join. Partake. Die.

SELENOTROPISM

A drop of my liniment oil
seeps into a remarkable

man's fingertip and is given

over after centuries of
microscopic exploration

to a wise tongue
and clear throat

swallowing like supplication
my keepsake nourishment.

GAINING PERSPECTIVE UP CLOSE
OF OUR FAR, FAR AWAY

And I like to look at you in daybreak,
when it's fair trade, crunch time, and man bags,
and I like to look at you in spices,
whether truffle-salt, oregano, or sumac,
and I like to look at you in Eastertime,
when it's anniversary lore and poppy lure,
and I like to look at you in colorfulness,
whether sapphire, bombshell, or polychromatic,
and I like to look at you in measure,
when it's passageway and high-def virility,
and I like to look at you in lucidness,
whether telescope, rearview, or referendum,
and I like to look at you in reflection,
when it's hand mirror, relics, or golden hour,
and I like to look at you in lamplight,
whether in the same sofa or across county lines,
and I like to look at you in intervals,
when it's racing sun or boxing snow,
and I like to look at you in granularity,
whether haze, graze, or sling-suspension,
and I like to look at you in planes,
when it's cosmos, stovetop, and eagle's nest,
and I like to look at you in subtext,
whether health, self, or wealth,
and I like to look at you in fruition,
when it's ameba, twerking, and globe,
and I like to look at you in the evening,
whether it's toothpaste, rancor, or tale,
and I like to look at you in slumber,
when it's the inversion of waking things,
and I like to look at you looking at me,
whether it's launch, midpoint, or game, set, match.

TRAVELLING LIGHT

Upon the foot bed of midnight,
when the goddess of descendancy

bows and asks me to name the
heaviest encumbrance from this

season of bereft, I will stand,
soul in my hands, and whisper

through the mistake-stains
embossed on my lips, love.

Grateful acknowledgment is made to the following journals, in which some of these poems first appeared in slightly different forms: Boomerlit, Split Rock Review, Pure Slush, Paragon Journal, Pomona Valley Review, Heart Online, and White Liquor. Grateful acknowledgment is made to Marc Pietrzykowski, who believed in this collection, and to The Minnesota Writers Workshop, Kurt Duex, Shauna Nyberg, Char Rutz, and Nicole and Brett Bundy, who loved me through the brokenness and helped me heal.

Samuel E. Cole lives in Woodbury, Minnesota.

Pski's Porch Publishing was formed July 2012, to make books for people who like people who like books. We hope we have some small successes.
www.pskisporch.com.

Pski's Porch

323 East Avenue
Lockport, NY 14094
www.pskisporch.com

www.ingramcontent.com/pod-product-compliance
Lightning Source LLC
LaVergne TN
LVHW051743080426
835511LV00018B/3205